DIVINE WORSHIP

PASTORAL CARE OF THE SICK AND DYING

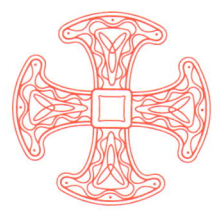

Published by
THE CATHOLIC TRUTH SOCIETY
40-46 Harleyford Road, London, SE11 5AY

ISBN 978 1 78469 639 9
RM37

Copyright © 2020 The Personal Ordinariate of the Chair of Saint Peter, the Personal Ordinariate of Our Lady of Walsingham, and the Personal Ordinariate of Our Lady of the Southern Cross.

Scripture readings from the *Revised Standard Version, Second Catholic Edition* © Ignatius Press.

Printed and bound by L.E.G.O. S.p.A., Italy.

CONTENTS

DIVINE WORSHIP: PASTORAL CARE OF THE SICK AND DYING

Decrees 4
Apostolic Constitution 9
General Introduction 17
Chapter 1. Visitation of the Sick. 21
Chapter 2. Blessing of a Sick Child. 31
Chapter 3. Communion of the Sick - Ordinary Rite. 37
Chapter 4. Communion of the Sick - Shorter Rite . . 49
Chapter 5. Anointing of the Sick Outside of Mass . . 55
Chapter 6. Penance, Anointing, and Viaticum 65
Chapter 7. Supplication for the Dying and Commendation of a Soul 77
Chapter 8. Additional Prayers which may be used with the foregoing. . 85
Appendix: Sacramental and Other Formulas 95
    Sacrament of Penance 95
    Anointing of the Sick. 97
    Viaticum 97
    Apostolic Pardon 97

CONGREGATIO PRO DOCTRINA FIDEI

Prot. N. 536/2012

CONGREGATIO PRO DOCTRINA FIDEI

DECRETUM

Medicus animarum corporumque nostrorum, Dominus Iesus Ecclesiam voluit sanationis salutisque opus, Spiritus Sancti virtute, perseverare et adusque, instar Boni Samaritani, hominem quemque infirmitate laborantem appropinquat, eius vulneribus consolationis oleum et spei vinum instillans.

Proinde, mentem in animarum bonum ac potissimum in aegrotos paterno animo advertens, ratione habita instantium pastoralium necessitatum, ad normam Constitutionis Apostolicae «Anglicanorum coetibus», n. 3, ubi facultas conceditur Sacramenta celebrandi iuxta libros liturgicos Anglicano patrimonio peculiares ab Apostolica Sede approbatos, textus *Ordinis unctionis infirmorum* lingua anglica exaratus, litteris die 7 iunii 2016 ad hanc Congregationem traditus, collatis consiliis Congregationis de Cultu Divino et Disciplina Sacramentorum, sicut in adiecto exstat exemplari ab ipso Summo Pontifice

FRANCISCO, in audientia infrascripto Congregationis pro Doctrina Fidei Cardinali Praefecto die 7 novembris 2019 concessa, probatus est.

De mandatu Summi Pontificis haec Congregatio pro Doctrina Fidei hoc Decretum publici iuris fecit.

Contrariis quibuslibet minime obstantibus.

Ex aedibus Congregationis pro Doctrina Fidei, die 11 novembris 2019, in memoria Sancti Martini Turonensis, episcopi.

Aloisius Franciscus Card. L<small>ADARIA</small>, S.I.
Praefectus

✠ Iacobus M<small>ORANDI</small>
Archiep. tit. Caeretanus
A Secretis

DIVINE WORSHIP: PASTORAL CARE OF THE SICK AND DYING

DECREE OF PUBLICATION FOR THE PERSONAL ORDINARIATE OF THE CHAIR OF SAINT PETER, THE PERSONAL ORDINARIATE OF OUR LADY OF WALSINGHAM, AND THE PERSONAL ORDINARIATE OF OUR LADY OF THE SOUTHERN CROSS

In accord with the norms established by the decree of the Sacred Congregation of Rites in *Cum, nostra aetate* (27 January 1966), this *Divine Worship: Pastoral Care of the Sick and Dying* is published by the authority of the Personal Ordinariate of the Chair of Saint Peter, the Personal Ordinariate of Our Lady of the Southern Cross, and the Personal Ordinariate of Our Lady of Walsingham.

Divine Worship: Pastoral Care of the Sick and Dying was canonically approved for use by the Personal Ordinariates established under the auspices of the Apostolic Constitution *Anglicanorum coetibus* by decree of the Congregation for the Doctrine of the Faith on 11 November 2019 (Prot. N. 536/2012). *Divine Worship: Pastoral Care of the Sick and Dying* may be used by the communities of the Personal

Ordinariate of the Chair of Saint Peter, the Personal Ordinariate of Our Lady of the Southern Cross, and the Personal Ordinariate of Our Lady of Walsingham from Sunday, 12 April 2020.

Given on 11 February, 2020, the Memorial of Our Lady of Lourdes.

☩ Most Rev. Steven J. Lopes, STD
Bishop, Personal Ordinariate of the
Chair of Saint Peter

Rev. Msgr. Carl Reid, PA
Ordinary,
Personal Ordinariate of
Our Lady of the Southern Cross

Rev. Msgr. Keith Newton, PA
Ordinary,
Personal Ordinariate of
Our Lady of Walsingham

APOSTOLIC CONSTITUTION OF POPE PAUL VI

SACRAM UNCTIONE INFIRMORUM

ON THE SACRAMENT
OF ANOINTING OF THE SICK

The Catholic Church professes and teaches that the Sacred Anointing of the Sick is one of the seven Sacraments of the New Testament, that it was instituted by Christ and that it is "alluded to in Mark (*Mk* 6:13) and recommended and promulgated to the faithful by James the apostle and brother of the Lord. If any one of you is ill, he says, he should send for the elders of the church, and they must anoint him with oil in the name of the Lord and pray over him. The prayer of faith will save the sick man and the Lord will raise him up again; and if he has committed any sins, he will be forgiven (*Jm* 5:14-15)."[1]

From ancient times testimonies of the Anointing of the Sick are found in the Church's Tradition, particularly her liturgical Tradition, both in the East and in the West. Especially worthy of note in this regard are the Letter which Innocent I, our predecessor, addressed to

---

[1] Council of Trent, Session XIV, *De Extrema Unctione*, chapter 1 (cf. ibid. canon 1): *CT*, VII, 1, 355-356; Denz. Schon., 1695, 1716.

Decentius, Bishop of Gubbio,[2] and the venerable prayer used for blessing the Oil of the Sick: "Send forth, O Lord, your Holy Spirit, the Paraclete," which was inserted in the Eucharistic Prayer[3] and is still preserved in the Roman Pontifical.[4]

In the course of the centuries, in the liturgical Tradition the parts of the body of the sick person to be anointed with Holy Oil were more explicitly defined, in different ways, and there were added various formulas to accompany the anointings with prayer, which are contained in the liturgical books of various Churches. During the Middle Ages, in the Roman Church there prevailed the custom of anointing the sick on the five senses, using the formula: *Per istam Sanctam unctionem*

---

[2] Pope Innocent I, Letter *Si Instituta Ecclesiastica*, chapter 8: PL, 20, 559-561; Denz. Schon., 216.

[3] *Liber Sacramentorum Romanae Ecclesiae Ordinis Anni Circuli*, ed. L. C. Mohlberg (*Rerum Ecclesiasticarum Documenta, Fontes*, IV), Rome 1960, p. 61; *Le Sacramentaire Gregorien*, ed. J. Deshusses (*Spicilegium Friburgense*, 16), Fribourg 1971, p. 172; cf. *La Tradition Apostolique de Saint Hippolyte*, ed. B. Botte (*Liturgiewissenschaftliche Quellen und Forschungen*, 39), Münster-W. 1963, pp. 18-19; *Le Grand Euchologe du Monastère Blanc*, ed. E. Lanne (*Patrologia Orientalis*, XXVIII, 2), Paris 1958, pp. 392-395.

[4] Cf. *Pontificale Romanum: Ordo benedicendi Oleum Catechumenorum et Infirmorum et conficiendi Chrisma*, Vatican City 1971, pp. 11-12.

et suam Piissimam misericordiam, indulgeat tibi Dominus quidquid deliquisti, adapted to each sense.[5]

In addition, the doctrine concerning Sacred Anointing is expounded in the documents of the Ecumenical Councils, namely the Council of Florence and in particular the Council of Trent and the Second Vatican Council.

After the Council of Florence had described the essential elements of the Anointing of the Sick,[6] the Council of Trent declared its divine institution and explained what is given in the Epistle of Saint James concerning the Sacred Anointing, especially with regard to the reality and effects of the sacrament: "This reality is in fact the grace of the Holy Spirit, whose anointing takes away sins, if any still remain to be taken away, and the remnants of sin; it also relieves and strengthens the soul of the sick person, arousing in him a great confidence in the divine mercy, whereby being thus sustained he more easily bears the trials and labours of his sickness, more easily resists the temptations of the devil 'lying in wait' (*Gen* 3:15), and sometimes regains bodily health, if

---

[5] Cf. M. Andrieu, *Le Pontifical Romain au Moyen-Age*, vol. 1, *Le Pontifical Romain du XIIe siècle* (*Studi e Testi*, 86), Vatican City 1938, pp. 267-268; vol. 2, *Le Pontifical de la Curie Romaine au XIIIe sieècle* (*Studi e Testi*, 87), Vatican City 1940 pp. 491-492.

[6] Council of Florence, *Decr. pro Armeniis*, G. Hofmann, *Concilium Florentinum* 1/11, p. 130; Denz. Schon.,1324f.

this is expedient for the health of the soul."[7] The same Council also declared that in these words of the Apostle it is stated with sufficient clarity that "this anointing is to be administered to the sick, especially those who are in such a condition as to appear to have reached the end of their life, whence it is also called the sacrament of the dying."[8] Finally, it declared that the priest is the proper minister of the sacrament.[9]

The Second Vatican Council adds the following: "'Extreme Unction,' which may also and more fittingly be called 'Anointing of the Sick,' is not a sacrament for those only who are at the point of death. Hence, as soon as any one of the faithful begins to be in danger of death from sickness or old age, the appropriate time for him to receive this sacrament has certainly already arrived."[10] The fact that the use of this sacrament concerns the whole Church is shown by these words: "By the sacred anointing of the sick and the prayer of her priests, the whole Church commends those who are ill to the suffering and glorified Lord, asking that he may lighten their suffering and save them (cf. *Jm* 5:14-16). She exhorts them, moreover, to contribute to the welfare of

---

[7] Council of Trent, Sess. XIV, *De Extrema Unctione*, chapter 2: CT, VII, 1, 356; Denz. Schon., 1696.

[8] Ibid., chapter 3: CT, ibid.; Denz. Schon., 1698.

[9] Ibid., chapter 3, canon 4: CT, ibid.; Denz. Schon., 1697-1719.

[10] Second Vatican Council, Const. *Sacrosanctum Concilium*, 73: A.A.S., LVI (1964) 118-119.

the whole People of God by associating themselves freely with the passion and death of Christ (cf. *Rom* 8:17; *Col* 1:24; *2 Tim* 2:11-12; *1 Pt* 4:13)."[11]

All these elements had to be taken into consideration in revising the rite of Sacred Anointing, in order better to adapt to present-day conditions those elements, which were subject to change.[12]

We thought fit to modify the sacramental formula in such a way that, in view of the words of Saint James, the effects of the sacrament might be better expressed.

Further, since olive oil, which hitherto had been prescribed for the valid administration of the sacrament, is unobtainable or difficult to obtain in some parts of the world, we decreed, at the request of numerous bishops, that in the future, according to the circumstances, oil of another sort could also be used, provided it were obtained from plants, inasmuch as this more closely resembles the matter indicated in Holy Scripture.

As regards the number of anointings and the parts of the body to be anointed, it has seemed to us opportune to proceed to a simplification of the rite. Therefore, since this revision in certain points touches upon the sacramental rite itself, by our Apostolic authority we lay down that the following is to be observed for the future in the Latin Rite:

---

[11] Ibid., Const. *Lumen Gentium*, II: A.A.S., LVII (1965) 15.

[12] Second Vatican Council, Const. *Sacrosanctum Concilium*, 1: A.A.S. LVI (1964) 97.

THE SACRAMENT OF THE ANOINTING OF THE SICK IS ADMINISTERED TO THOSE WHO ARE DANGEROUSLY ILL, BY ANOINTING THEM ON THE FOREHEAD AND HANDS WITH OLIVE OIL, OR, IF OPPORTUNE, WITH ANOTHER VEGETABLE OIL, PROPERLY BLESSED, AND SAYING ONCE ONLY THE FOLLOWING WORDS:

THROUGH THIS HOLY ANOINTING

MAY THE LORD IN HIS LOVE AND MERCY HELP YOU

WITH THE GRACE OF THE HOLY SPIRIT.

MAY THE LORD WHO FREES YOU FROM SIN

SAVE YOU AND RAISE YOU UP.

[PER ISTAM SANCTAM UNCTIONEM ET SUAM PIISSIMAM MISERICORDIAM ADIUVET TE DOMINUS GRATIA SPIRITUS SANCTI, UT A PECCATIS LIBERATUM TE SALVET ATQUE PROPITIUS ALLEVIET.]

In case of necessity however it is sufficient that a single anointing be given on the forehead or, because of the particular condition of the sick person, on another more suitable part of the body, the whole formula being pronounced.

This sacrament can be repeated if the sick person, having once received the Anointing, recovers and then again falls sick, or if, in the course of the same illness, the danger becomes more acute.

Having laid down and declared these elements concerning the essential rite of the sacrament of the Anointing of the Sick, we, by our Apostolic authority, also approve the Order of the Anointing of the Sick and of their pastoral care, as it has been revised by the Sacred Congregation for Divine Worship. At the same time, we revoke, where necessary, the prescriptions of the Code of Canon Law or other laws hitherto in force, or we abrogate them; other prescriptions and laws, which are neither abrogated nor changed by the above-mentioned Order, remain valid and in force. The Latin edition of the Order containing the new rite will come into force as soon as it is published. The vernacular editions, prepared by the episcopal conferences and confirmed by the Apostolic See, will come into force on the day that will be laid down by the individual conferences. The old Order can be used until December 31, 1973. From January 1, 1974, however, the new Order only is to be used by all those whom it concerns.

We desire that these decrees and prescriptions of ours shall, now and in the future, be fully effective in the Latin Rite, notwithstanding, as far as is necessary, the Apostolic Constitutions and Directives issued by our predecessors and other prescriptions, even if worthy of special mention.

Given at St Peter's in Rome, on the thirtieth day of November, in the year 1972, the tenth of our Pontificate.

PAUL VI, POPE

DIVINE WORSHIP:
PASTORAL CARE OF THE SICK AND DYING

GENERAL INTRODUCTION

1. "By the sacred anointing of the sick and the prayer of the priests the whole Church commends those who are ill to the suffering and glorifed Lord, that he may raise them up and save them. And indeed she exhorts them to contribute to the good of the People of God by freely uniting themselves to the Passion and death of Christ."[1] The Sacrament of Anointing, instituted by Christ and celebrated by the Church from Apostolic times (cf. *Jm* 5:14-16), expressed the Lord's own concern for the bodily and spiritual welfare of the sick.

2. *Divine Worship: Pastoral Care of the Sick and Dying*, for use by the Ordinariates erected under the auspices of the Apostolic Constitution *Anglicanorum coetibus*, gives expression to Anglican liturgical patrimony which has nourished many in their faith in the forgiveness of sins and strengthening of the soul and body through the sacramental ministry entrusted to the Church. Its use is

---

[1] Catechism of the Catholic Church, 1499. Cf. also Second Vatican Council, *Lumen Gentium*, 11.

restricted to the Personal Ordinariates established under the Apostolic Constitution *Anglicanorum coetibus*.[2]

3. In cases of pastoral necessity or in the absence of a Priest incardinated in an Ordinariate, any Priest incardinated in a Diocese or Institute of Consecrated Life or Society of Apostolic Life may celebrate the sacrament of Anointing of the Sick according to *Divine Worship: Pastoral Care of the Sick and Dying* for members of the Ordinariate who request it.

4. As a liturgical provision for the sanctification of the faithful who come to the Catholic Church from the Anglican tradition, *Divine Worship: Pastoral Care of the Sick and Dying* presents the appropriate texts from *Divine Worship: The Missal*, applying them for the particular circumstance of the administration of Holy Communion to sick persons in their homes, in hospitals, or in other settings outside of Mass. The sacramental formulae for the Sacrament of Anointing and the Sacrament of Penance as presented here are identical with those of the Roman Rite of the Catholic Church and may not be modified or amended in any way.

5. The liturgical norms and principles of the Roman Ritual, *Pastoral Care of the Sick: Rites of Anointing and*

---

[2] Cf. Pope Benedict XVI, Apostolic Constitution *Anglicanorum coetibus*, Art. III.

Viaticum, are normative for this expression of the Roman Rite. For any circumstances that are not covered in this current Order, reference should be made to the normative Roman Ritual, *Pastoral Care of the Sick: Rites of Anointing and Viaticum.*

6. The Priest is the only proper minister of the Sacrament of the Anointing of the Sick.[3] The Sacrament of Anointing is the proper sacrament for those Catholics who have attained the age of reason and whose health is seriously impaired by sickness, old age, or impending surgery.

7. The ordinary Minister of the Communion of the Sick is most fittingly a Priest, but a Deacon may also administer Communion to the sick. A layperson designated as an Extraordinary Minister of Holy Communion may take the Sacrament to the sick but more appropriately does so according to the Shorter Rite for Communion of the Sick.

8. The use of "Holy Ghost" in place of "Holy Spirit" is permitted according to local custom.

---

[3] Cf. Code of Canon Law, Can. 1006.

CHAPTER ONE:
VISITATION OF THE SICK

Outline of the Rite

>Introductory Rites
>Psalmody
>Profession of Faith
>Laying on of Hands
>Blessing of the Sick

Introductory Rites

9. In the office following, a lay minister shall omit those parts reserved to a Priest or Deacon. The responses are to be made by the sick person and those assembled with him or her.

On entering the house or room, the Minister says:

>Peace be to this house, and to all that dwell in it.

People: **Amen.**

>Or, a Priest or Deacon may say:

>The peace of the Lord be always with you.

People: **And with thy spirit.**

The Minister may recite one or more of these Sentences:

The eternal God is thy refuge, and underneath are the everlasting arms. (*Deuteronomy 33:27*)

They that wait upon the Lord shall renew their strength. (*Isaiah 40:31*)

In nothing be anxious: but in everything, by prayer and supplication with thanksgiving, let your requests be made known unto God. And the peace of God, which passeth all understanding, shall keep your hearts and minds in Christ Jesus. *(Philippians 4:6-7)*

Then the Minister shall say:

>Let us pray.
>
>Lord, have mercy upon us.

People: **Christ, have mercy upon us.**
Minister: Lord have mercy upon us.

Minister and People together:

OUR Father, who art in heaven, hallowed be thy Name, thy kingdom come, thy will be done, on earth as it is in heaven. Give us this day our daily bread. And forgive us our trespasses, as we forgive those who trespass against us. And lead us not into temptation, but deliver us from evil. Amen.

Minister: O Lord, save thy servant;
People: **Who putteth his (her) trust in thee.**

Minister: Send him (her) help from thy holy place;
People: **And evermore mightily defend him (her).**

Minister: Let the enemy have no advantage of him (her);
People: **Nor the wicked approach to hurt him (her).**

Minister: Be unto him (her), O Lord, a strong tower;
People: **From the face of his (her) enemy.**
Minister: O Lord, hear our prayer.
People: **And let our cry come unto thee.**

The Minister continues:

GOD of all grace and power: behold, visit, and relieve thy servant N.; look upon him (her) with the eyes of thy mercy; give him (her) comfort and sure confidence in thee, defend him (her) in all danger, and keep him (her) in perpetual peace and safety; through Jesus Christ thy Son our Lord, who liveth and reigneth with thee, in the unity of the Holy Spirit, ever one God, world without end. **Amen.**

Psalmody

10. Then shall the Minister and People together say one of the following psalms, with this antiphon before and after:

Ant. O Saviour of the world, who by thy Cross and precious Blood hast redeemed us: **Save us, and help us, we humbly beseech thee, O Lord.**

Psalm 23. *Dominus regit me.*

THE LORD is my shepherd; * therefore can I lack nothing.

He shall feed me in a green pasture, * and lead me forth beside the waters of comfort.

He shall convert my soul, * and bring me forth in the paths of righteousness for his Name's sake.

Yea, though I walk through the valley of the shadow of death, I will fear no evil; * for thou art with me; thy rod and thy staff comfort me.

Thou shalt prepare a table before me in the presence of them that trouble me; * thou hast anointed my head with oil, and my cup shall be full.

Surely thy loving-kindness and mercy shall follow me all the days of my life; * and I will dwell in the house of the LORD for ever.

Glory be to the Father, and to the Son, and to the Holy Ghost; as it was in the beginning, is now, and ever shall be, world without end. Amen.

Or:

Psalm 121. *Levavi oculos.*

I WILL lift up mine eyes unto the hills; * from whence cometh my help?

My help cometh even from the LORD, * who hath made heaven and earth.

He will not suffer thy foot to be moved; * and he that keepeth thee will not sleep.

Behold, he that keepeth Israel * shall neither slumber nor sleep.

The LORD himself is thy keeper; * the LORD is thy defence upon thy right hand;

So that the sun shall not burn thee by day, * neither the moon by night.

The LORD shall preserve thee from all evil; * yea, it is even he that shall keep thy soul.

The LORD shall preserve thy going out, and thy coming in, * from this time forth for evermore.

Glory be to the Father, and to the Son, and to the Holy Ghost; as it was in the beginning, is now, and ever shall be, world without end. Amen.

Ant. O Saviour of the world, who by thy Cross and precious Blood hast redeemed us: **Save us, and help us, we humbly beseech thee, O Lord.**

Profession of Faith

11. If time allows and if the condition of the sick person permits, the baptismal profession of faith follows. The Minister first says and then asks the following questions:

Let us profess our faith in the redeeming love of God.

N., do you believe in God the Father Almighty, Maker of heaven and earth?

Sick person: **I do.**

Minister: Do you believe in Jesus Christ, his only Son our Lord, who was conceived by the Holy Ghost, born of the Virgin Mary, suffered under Pontius Pilate, was crucified, dead, and buried; he descended into hell; the third day he rose again from the dead; he ascended into heaven, and sitteth on the right hand of God the Father Almighty; from thence he shall come to judge the quick and the dead?

Sick person: **I do.**

Minister: Do you believe in the Holy Ghost; the holy Catholic Church; the Communion of Saints; the forgiveness of sins, the resurrection of the body, and the life everlasting?

Sick person: **All this I steadfastly believe.**

If a Priest conducts the visitation, he may then approach the sick person in order to ascertain if the person wishes to make his (her) confession. If so, the Priest, wearing a violet stole, shall hear his (her) confession and give absolution.

VISITATION OF THE SICK

Laying on of Hands

12. If appropriate, the Priest may then celebrate the Sacrament of the Anointing of the Sick (cf. pp. 55-63.). Otherwise the Priest or Deacon may simply place his right hand on the sick person, saying:

I lay my hands upon thee, In the Name of the Father, and of the Son, and of the Holy Spirit.

The Priest or Deacon continues:

O ALMIGHTY God, whose blessed Son did lay his hands upon the sick and healed them: grant, we beseech thee, to this person on whom we now lay our hand in his Name, refreshment of spirit and, if it be thy will, perfect restoration to health; through the same Jesus Christ thy Son our Lord. Amen.

Or:

MAY Jesus, the Son of Mary, the Lord and Redeemer of the world, through the merits and intercession of his holy Apostles Peter and Paul, and of all his Saints, show thee favour and mercy. Amen.

Blessing of the Sick

13. The Priest or Deacon may then bless the sick person as follows:

V. Our help is in the Name of the Lord.
R. **Who hath made heaven and earth.**

V. Who himself took our infirmities;
R. **And bore our sicknesses.**

V. The Lord be with you.
R. **And with thy spirit.**

Let us pray.

ALMIGHTY and immortal God, the giver of life and health: We beseech thee to hear our prayers for thy servant N., for whom we implore thy mercy, that by thy blessing upon him (her) and upon those who minister to him (her) of thy healing gifts, he (she) may be restored, according to thy gracious will, to health of body and mind, and give thanks to thee in thy holy Church; through Jesus Christ our Lord. **Amen.**

The blessing of God Almighty, ✠ the Father, the Son, and the Holy Ghost, descend upon thee, work thy healing, and remain with thee always. **Amen.**

VISITATION OF THE SICK

Otherwise, the office shall conclude as follows, the Minister saying:

THE Almighty Lord, who is a most strong tower to all those who put their trust in him, to whom all things in heaven, in earth, and under the earth, do bow and obey; be now and evermore thy defence; and make thee know and feel, that there is none other Name under heaven given to man, in whom, and through whom, thou mayest receive health and salvation, but only the Name of our Lord Jesus Christ. **Amen.**

A lay minister may say, while tracing the Sign of the Cross on the sick person's forehead:

UNTO God's gracious mercy and protection we commit thee. The Lord bless thee, and keep thee. The Lord make his face to shine upon thee, and be gracious unto thee. The Lord lift up his countenance upon thee, and give thee peace, both now and evermore. **Amen.**

CHAPTER TWO:
BLESSING OF A SICK CHILD

Outline of the Rite

Psalmody
Laying on of Hands and Blessing

14. The ordinary Minister of the Blessing of a Sick Child is a Priest, Deacon, or a designated layperson chosen for the ministry of the sick. In the rite following, a lay minister shall omit those parts reserved to a Priest or Deacon. The responses are to be made by the sick child, if able so to do, and those assembled with him or her.

On entering the house or room, the Minister says:

>Peace be to this house, and to all that dwell in it.

People: **Amen.**

Or, a Priest or Deacon may say:

>The peace of the Lord be always with you.

People: **And with thy spirit.**

If a Priest officiates, wearing a white stole, he may sprinkle the sick child, the bed, and the room with holy water, saying nothing.

Psalmody

Then shall the Minister say over the sick child:

Psalm 113. *Laudate, pueri.*

PRAISE the LORD, ye servants; * O praise the Name of the LORD.

Blessed be the Name of the LORD * from this time forth for evermore.

The LORD'S Name is praised * from the rising up of the sun unto the going down of the same.

The LORD is high above all nations, * and his glory above the heavens.

Who is like unto the LORD our God, that hath his dwelling so high, * and yet humbleth himself to behold the things that are in heaven and earth!

He taketh up the simple out of the dust, * and lifteth the poor out of the mire;

That he may set him with the princes, * even with the princes of his people.

He maketh the barren woman to keep house, * and to be a joyful mother of children.

Glory be to the Father, and to the Son, and to the Holy Ghost; as it was in the beginning, is now, and ever shall be, world without end. Amen.

BLESSING OF A SICK CHILD

Minister: Lord, have mercy upon us.
People: **Christ, have mercy upon us.**
Minister: Lord have mercy upon us.

Minister and People together:

OUR Father, who art in heaven, hallowed be thy Name, thy kingdom come, thy will be done, on earth as it is in heaven. Give us this day our daily bread. And forgive us our trespasses, as we forgive those who trespass against us. And lead us not into temptation, but deliver us from evil. Amen.

V. Be merciful, O our God.
R. **Defend the children, O Lord.**

V. Suffer the little children to come unto me.
R. **For of such is the kingdom of heaven.**

V. O Lord, hear my prayer.
R. **And let my cry come unto thee.**

A Priest or Deacon adds:

V. The Lord be with you.
R. **And with thy spirit.**

Let us pray.

O LORD Jesus Christ, who didst with joy receive and bless the children brought unto thee: give thy blessing to this child; and in thine own time deliver him (her) from his (her) illness, that he (she) may live to serve thee all his (her) days. **Amen.**

O EVERLASTING God, who hast ordained and constituted the services of Angels and men in a wonderful order: mercifully grant that, as thy holy Angels always do serve thee in heaven, so, by thy appointment, they may succour and defend this thy child on earth; through Jesus Christ thy Son our Lord. **Amen.**

Laying on of Hands and Blessing

15. If a Priest or Deacon conducts the office, he shall then lay his right hand on the head of the sick child, saying:

I lay my hands upon thee, In the Name of the Father, and of the Son, and of the Holy Spirit.

The Priest or Deacon continues:

O ALMIGHTY God, whose blessed Son did lay his hands upon the sick and healed them: grant, we beseech thee, to this child on whom we now lay our hands in his Name, refreshment of spirit and, if it be thy will, perfect restoration to health; through the same Jesus Christ thy Son our Lord. **Amen.**

Or:

MAY Jesus, the Son of Mary, the Lord and Redeemer of the world, through the merits and intercession of his holy Apostles Peter and Paul, and of all his Saints, show thee favour and mercy. **Amen.**

BLESSING OF A SICK CHILD

And blessing the sick child he shall say:

The blessing of God Almighty, ✠ the Father, the Son, and the Holy Ghost, descend upon thee, work thy healing, and remain with thee always. Amen.

Then he may sprinkle the child with holy water.

In the absence of a Priest or Deacon, the office shall conclude as follows, the Minister saying:

O GOD, in whom all things grow, and by whom all that which is come to full stature is made strong: stretch forth thy right hand upon this thy child who, at this tender age, is stricken with sickness; and grant, that being restored to health and strength, he (she) may attain to fulness of years and may serve thee faithfully and thankfully all the days of his (her) life; through Jesus Christ thy Son our Lord. **Amen.**

Or:

LORD Jesus Christ, Good Shepherd of the sheep, who gatherest the lambs in thine arms and carriest them in thy bosom: we commend to thy loving care this child N.; relieve his (her) pain, guard him (her) from all danger, restore to him (her) thy gifts of gladness and strength, and raise him (her) up to a life of faithful service to thee; through Jesus Christ thy Son our Lord. **Amen.**

A lay minister, or preferably the child's parents, may say, while tracing the Sign of the Cross on the child's forehead:

UNTO God's gracious mercy and protection we commit thee. The Lord bless thee, and keep thee. The Lord make his face to shine upon thee, and be gracious unto thee. The Lord lift up his countenance upon thee, and give thee peace, both now and evermore. **Amen.**

CHAPTER THREE:
COMMUNION OF THE SICK

ORDINARY RITE

Outline of the Rite

>Introductory Rites
>Penitential Rite
>Liturgy of the Word
>Rite of Holy Communion
>Blessing
>Reposition of the Blessed Sacrament

16. The Priest or Deacon should arrange the visit with the sick person, or caregivers, in advance. He should instruct them about the reverence due the Blessed Sacrament, including the necessity of due spiritual preparation. He should ascertain how many people intend to receive Holy Communion during the visit. If it is at all possible, the following should be prepared in the room before the arrival of the Priest or Deacon: a table covered with a fair linen cloth, or else a decent white covering, having upon it two candles, or at least one, and a crucifix. The Priest or Deacon should bring not only the Blessed Sacrament, in a pyx, but also a corporal, a purificator, and a vessel of water, and, if convenient and customary, also a vessel containing holy water to be sprinkled.

When the sick person is himself a Priest or Deacon, it is fitting that he be vested for Holy Communion in a white stole.

The Priest who carries the Blessed Sacrament should be vested in a surplice and white stole, or at least a stole. He may additionally require a violet stole if the sick person wishes to make a confession.

Introductory Rites

17. On entering the house or room, the Minister says:

>Peace be to this house, and to all that dwell in it.

People: **Amen.**

Or, a Priest or Deacon may say:

>The peace of the Lord be always with you.

People: **And with thy spirit.**

18. Next the Priest or Deacon may take the vessel of holy water and sprinkle the sick person and room, saying:

Thou shalt purge me with hyssop, O Lord, and I shall be clean; thou shalt wash me, and I shall be whiter than snow.

Minister: Our help is in the Name of the Lord.
People: **Who hath made heaven and earth.**

Minister: O Lord, hear my prayer.
People: **And let my cry come unto thee.**

A Priest or Deacon adds:

>The Lord be with you.

People: **And with thy spirit.**

Minister: Let us pray.

O LORD, holy Father, Almighty, everlasting God, we beseech thee to hear us; and vouchsafe to send thy holy Angel from heaven, to guard and cherish, protect and visit, and evermore defend all who are assembled in this place; through Christ our Lord. **Amen.**

COMMUNION OF THE SICK

Penitential Rite

19. The Priest may then approach the sick person in order to ascertain if the person wishes to make his (her) confession. If so, wearing a violet stole, he shall hear his (her) confession and give absolution.

Unless the Sacrament of Penance has been celebrated, the Priest or Deacon shall then proceed with the Penitential Rite:

Ye that do truly and earnestly repent you of your sins, and are in love and charity with your neighbours, and intend to lead a new life, following the commandments of God, and walking from henceforth in his holy ways: draw near with faith, and make your humble confession to almighty God, meekly kneeling upon your knees.

Or:

Let us humbly confess our sins unto Almighty God.

The People kneel, if they are able. Silence may be kept, and then the Priest or Deacon begins as follows and the People join in saying:

ALMIGHTY God,
Father of our Lord Jesus Christ,
maker of all things, judge of all men:

**We acknowledge and bewail our manifold sins and wickedness,
which we from time to time most grievously have committed,**

by thought, word, and deed, against thy divine majesty,
provoking most justly thy wrath and indignation
against us.

We do earnestly repent,
and are heartily sorry for these our misdoings;
the remembrance of them is grievous unto us,
the burden of them is intolerable.

Have mercy upon us,
have mercy upon us, most merciful Father;
for thy Son our Lord Jesus Christ's sake,
forgive us all that is past;
and grant that we may ever hereafter
serve and please thee in newness of life,
to the honour and glory of thy Name;
through Jesus Christ our Lord. Amen.

The Priest says:

May Almighty God, our heavenly Father, who of his great mercy hath promised forgiveness of sins to all those who with hearty repentance and true faith turn unto him, have mercy on us, pardon and deliver us from all our sins, confirm and strengthen us in all goodness, and bring us to everlasting life; through Jesus Christ our Lord. Amen.

COMMUNION OF THE SICK

Then the Priest or Deacon says Let us pray, and the Collect of the Day (as appointed in the Missal), or else this Collect for the Sick:

GOD of all grace and power: behold, visit, and relieve thy servant N.; look upon him (her) with the eyes of thy mercy; give him (her) comfort and sure confidence in thee, defend him (her) in all danger, and keep him (her) in perpetual peace and safety; through Jesus Christ thy Son our Lord, who liveth and reigneth with thee, in the unity of the Holy Spirit, ever one God, world without end.

The People respond: **Amen.**

Liturgy of the Word

20. One or more texts from the Scriptures may then be read by one of those present or by the Minister. The reading from the Gospel shall be proclaimed by the Deacon or Priest. The readings may be those of the day (as appointed in the Lectionary) or these below.

A reading (or lesson) from the Second Letter of Saint Paul to the Corinthians. 2 Cor 4:1,16-18

Brethren: Having this ministry by the mercy of God, we do not lose heart. Though our outer nature is wasting away, our inner nature is being renewed every day. For this slight momentary affliction is preparing for us an eternal weight of glory beyond all comparison, because we look not to the things that are seen but to the things that are unseen; for the things that are seen are transient, but the things that are unseen are eternal.

Or:

A reading (or lesson) from the Letter of Saint James. 5:13-16

Beloved: Is any one among you suffering? Let him pray. Is any cheerful? Let him sing praise. Is any among you sick? Let him call for the elders of the church, and let them pray over him, anointing him with oil in the name of the Lord; and the prayer of faith will save the sick man, and the Lord will raise him up; and if he has committed sins, he will be forgiven. Therefore confess your sins to one another, and pray for one another, that you may be healed. The prayer of a righteous man has great power in its effects.

COMMUNION OF THE SICK

At the conclusion, the reader says:

> The Word of the Lord.

People: **Thanks be to God.**

If there is a reading before the Gospel, the following Gradual may be said: *Salvum fac* (Ps. 86:2b,6)

My God, save thy servant that putteth his trust in thee.

V. Give ear, Lord, unto my prayer.

Then, all standing who are able, the Deacon or Priest proclaims the Gospel, first saying with hands joined:

> The Lord be with you.

People: **And with thy spirit.**

A reading from the holy Gospel according to _____.

People: **Glory be to thee, O Lord.**

If the Gospel of the Day is not read, one of the following may be proclaimed:

A reading from the holy Gospel according to John.   5:24

Jesus said, "Truly, truly, I say to you, he who hears my word and believes him who sent me, has eternal life; he does not come into judgement, but has passed from death to life."

Or:

A reading from the holy Gospel according to John. 6:51

Jesus said to them, "I am the living bread which came down from heaven; if any one eats of this bread, he will live for ever; and the bread which I shall give for the life of the world is my flesh."

After the Gospel, the Deacon or Priest says:

>The Gospel of the Lord.

People: **Praise be to thee, O Christ.**

Then he kisses the book, saying quietly:

Through the words of the Gospel may our sins be blotted out.

The Priest or Deacon may give a brief reflection or a homily on the Gospel reading.

Rite of Holy Communion

21. The Priest or Deacon joins his hands to say:

As our Saviour Christ hath commanded and taught us, we are bold to say,

And here he extends his hands and begins the Lord's Prayer, as the People continue with him:

OUR Father, who art in heaven, hallowed be thy Name, thy kingdom come, thy will be done, on

COMMUNION OF THE SICK

earth as it is in heaven. Give us this day our daily bread. And forgive us our trespasses, as we forgive those who trespass against us. And lead us not into temptation, but deliver us from evil. Amen.

Then the Priest or Deacon, bowing profoundly, may say with all who shall receive Communion:

WE do not presume to come to this thy Table,
O merciful Lord, trusting in our own righteousness,
but in thy manifold and great mercies.

We are not worthy so much as to gather up the crumbs under thy Table.

But thou art the same Lord whose property is always to have mercy.

Grant us therefore, gracious Lord,
so to eat the flesh of thy dear Son Jesus Christ,
and to drink his Blood,
that our sinful bodies may be made clean by his Body,
and our souls washed through his most precious Blood,
and that we may evermore dwell in him, and he in us.
  Amen.

The Priest or Deacon genuflects, takes the Host and, turning to the People, holding it slightly raised above the pyx, says aloud:

Behold the Lamb of God, behold him that taketh away the sins of the world. Blessed are those who are called to the Supper of the Lamb.

The People respond together with him, once or three times:

Lord, I am not worthy that thou shouldest come under my roof, but speak the word only, and my soul shall be healed.

Then he distributes Holy Communion with these words:

The Body of our Lord Jesus Christ, which was given for thee, preserve thy body and soul unto everlasting life.

Or:

The Body of Christ.

When the distribution of Holy Communion is over, the Priest or Deacon purifies the pyx, unless he is to go immediately to another sick person and the Blessed Sacrament remains in the vessel.

After Communion, silence may be kept.

22. Then the Priest or Deacon standing and the People kneeling, if they are able, the Priest or Deacon alone, or all together, may say the following:

ALMIGHTY and everliving God,
  we most heartily thank thee for that thou dost feed us,
in these holy mysteries,
with the spiritual food of the most precious Body and Blood
of thy Son our Saviour Jesus Christ;

COMMUNION OF THE SICK

and dost assure us thereby
of thy favour and goodness towards us;

and that we are very members incorporate
in the mystical body of thy Son,
the blessed company of all faithful people;

and are also heirs, through hope,
of thy everlasting kingdom,
by the merits of the most precious death and Passion
of thy dear Son.

And we humbly beseech thee, O heavenly Father,
so to assist us with thy grace,
that we may continue in that holy fellowship,
and do all such good works
as thou hast prepared for us to walk in;

through Jesus Christ our Lord,
to whom, with thee and the Holy Spirit,
be all honour and glory, world without end. Amen.

Then the Priest or Deacon says Let us pray and the Postcommunion Prayer:

O LORD, holy Father almighty, everlasting God, we faithfully beseech thee that the most sacred Body of our Lord Jesus Christ thy Son, which our brother (sister) hath received, may avail for the everlasting healing both of body and soul; through Jesus Christ our Lord.

The People respond: **Amen.**

The Minister may then say the Collect of the Day, or one of the Prayers for the Sick (from the section of Additional Prayers, pg. 85) as appropriate to the person's circumstances and condition.

26. If time permits and it seems suitable, the Minister may read a text of Scripture (as set out in Communion of the Sick: Ordinary Rite).

Rite of Holy Communion

27. Then shall the Minister lead the sick person and those assembled in saying the Lord's Prayer:

As our Saviour Christ hath commanded and taught us, we are bold to say,

Minister and People together:

OUR Father, who art in heaven, hallowed be thy Name, thy kingdom come, thy will be done, on earth as it is in heaven. Give us this day our daily bread. And forgive us our trespasses, as we forgive those who trespass against us. And lead us not into temptation, but deliver us from evil. Amen.

The Minister then genuflects before the pyx laid on the table, removes the Host from the pyx, shows it to the sick person and those assembled, saying:

Behold the Lamb of God, behold him that taketh away the sins of the world. Blessed are those who are called to the Supper of the Lamb.

COMMUNION OF THE SICK

and dost assure us thereby
of thy favour and goodness towards us;

and that we are very members incorporate
in the mystical body of thy Son,
the blessed company of all faithful people;

and are also heirs, through hope,
of thy everlasting kingdom,
by the merits of the most precious death and Passion
of thy dear Son.

And we humbly beseech thee, O heavenly Father,
so to assist us with thy grace,
that we may continue in that holy fellowship,
and do all such good works
as thou hast prepared for us to walk in;

through Jesus Christ our Lord,
to whom, with thee and the Holy Spirit,
be all honour and glory, world without end. Amen.

Then the Priest or Deacon says Let us pray and the Postcommunion Prayer:

O LORD, holy Father almighty, everlasting God, we faithfully beseech thee that the most sacred Body of our Lord Jesus Christ thy Son, which our brother (sister) hath received, may avail for the everlasting healing both of body and soul; through Jesus Christ our Lord.

The People respond: **Amen.**

Blessing

23. Then, in silence, the Priest may give a blessing by making, with the pyx, the Sign of the Cross. Otherwise the blessing is given verbally, as usual:

The Priest says:

    The Lord be with you.

People: **And with thy spirit.**

The peace of God, which passeth all understanding, keep your hearts and minds in the knowledge and love of God, and of his Son Jesus Christ our Lord; and the blessing of God Almighty, ✢ the Father, the Son, and the Holy Spirit, be amongst you, and remain with you always.

People: **Amen.**

Reposition of the Blessed Sacrament

24. If he returns the Blessed Sacrament to the tabernacle, upon arriving at the altar he places the pyx upon an unfolded corporal on the altar, genuflects, and says:

Thou gavest them bread from heaven. (Alleluia.): Containing in itself all sweetness. (Alleluia.)

Let us pray.

O GOD, who in a wonderful Sacrament hast left unto us a memorial of thy Passion: grant us, we beseech thee, so to venerate the sacred mysteries of thy Body and Blood; that we may ever know within ourselves the fruit of thy redemption; who livest and reignest with the Father, in the unity of the Holy Spirit, ever one God, world without end. Amen.

CHAPTER FOUR: COMMUNION OF THE SICK

SHORTER RITE

Outline of the Rite

Introductory Rites
(Liturgy of the Word)
Rite of Holy Communion
Blessing
Reposition of the Blessed Sacrament

Introductory Rites

25. On entering the house or room, the Minister says:

> Peace be to this house, and to all that dwell in it.

People: **Amen.**

Or, a Priest or Deacon may say:

> The peace of the Lord be always with you.

People: **And with thy spirit.**

Then the Minister may say the following antiphon:

O sacred banquet! in which Christ is received, the memory of his Passion is renewed, the mind is filled with grace, and a pledge of future glory to us is given.

The Minister may then say the Collect of the Day, or one of the Prayers for the Sick (from the section of Additional Prayers, pg. 85) as appropriate to the person's circumstances and condition.

26. If time permits and it seems suitable, the Minister may read a text of Scripture (as set out in Communion of the Sick: Ordinary Rite).

Rite of Holy Communion

27. Then shall the Minister lead the sick person and those assembled in saying the Lord's Prayer:

As our Saviour Christ hath commanded and taught us, we are bold to say,

Minister and People together:

OUR Father, who art in heaven, hallowed be thy Name, thy kingdom come, thy will be done, on earth as it is in heaven. Give us this day our daily bread. And forgive us our trespasses, as we forgive those who trespass against us. And lead us not into temptation, but deliver us from evil. Amen.

The Minister then genuflects before the pyx laid on the table, removes the Host from the pyx, shows it to the sick person and those assembled, saying:

Behold the Lamb of God, behold him that taketh away the sins of the world. Blessed are those who are called to the Supper of the Lamb.

COMMUNION OF THE SICK - SHORTER RITE

The People respond together with the Minister, once or three times:

Lord, I am not worthy that thou shouldest come under my roof, but speak the word only, and my soul shall be healed.

Then shall the Minister distribute Holy Communion to the sick person, and to any assembled who are properly disposed to receive, with these words:

The Body of our Lord Jesus Christ, which was given for thee, preserve thy body and soul unto everlasting life.

Or:

The Body of Christ.

When the distribution of Holy Communion is over, the Minister purifies the pyx, unless he is to go immediately to another sick person and the Blessed Sacrament remains in the vessel.

After Communion, silence may be kept.

Then the Minister says Let us pray *and the Postcommunion Prayer:*

O LORD, holy Father almighty, everlasting God, we faithfully beseech thee that the most sacred Body of our Lord Jesus Christ thy Son, which our brother (sister) hath received, may avail for the everlasting healing both of body and soul; through Jesus Christ our Lord.

The People respond: **Amen.**

Blessing

28. Then, if a Priest be the Minister, he may give the blessing by making, with the pyx, in silence, the Sign of the Cross. Otherwise the blessing is given verbally, as usual:

The Priest says:

> The Lord be with you.

People: **And with thy spirit.**

The peace of God, which passeth all understanding, keep your hearts and minds in the knowledge and love of God, and of his Son Jesus Christ our Lord; and the blessing of God Almighty, ✠ the Father, the Son, and the Holy Spirit, be amongst you, and remain with you always.

People: **Amen.**

In the absence of a Priest or Deacon, the Minister shall conclude as follows:

THE Almighty Lord, who is a most strong tower to all those who put their trust in him, to whom all things in heaven, in earth, and under the earth, do bow and obey; be now and evermore thy defence; and make thee know and feel, that there is none other Name under heaven given to man, in whom, and through whom, thou mayest receive health and salvation, but only the Name of our Lord Jesus Christ. **Amen.**

CHAPTER FOUR: COMMUNION OF THE SICK

SHORTER RITE

Outline of the Rite

>Introductory Rites
>(Liturgy of the Word)
>Rite of Holy Communion
>Blessing
>Reposition of the Blessed Sacrament

Introductory Rites

25. On entering the house or room, the Minister says:

>Peace be to this house, and to all that dwell in it.

People: **Amen.**

Or, a Priest or Deacon may say:

>The peace of the Lord be always with you.

People: **And with thy spirit.**

Then the Minister may say the following antiphon:

O sacred banquet! in which Christ is received, the memory of his Passion is renewed, the mind is filled with grace, and a pledge of future glory to us is given.

The Minister may then say the Collect of the Day, or one of the Prayers for the Sick (from the section of Additional Prayers, pg. 85) as appropriate to the person's circumstances and condition.

26. If time permits and it seems suitable, the Minister may read a text of Scripture (as set out in Communion of the Sick: Ordinary Rite).

Rite of Holy Communion

27. Then shall the Minister lead the sick person and those assembled in saying the Lord's Prayer:

As our Saviour Christ hath commanded and taught us, we are bold to say,

Minister and People together:

OUR Father, who art in heaven, hallowed be thy Name, thy kingdom come, thy will be done, on earth as it is in heaven. Give us this day our daily bread. And forgive us our trespasses, as we forgive those who trespass against us. And lead us not into temptation, but deliver us from evil. Amen.

The Minister then genuflects before the pyx laid on the table, removes the Host from the pyx, shows it to the sick person and those assembled, saying:

Behold the Lamb of God, behold him that taketh away the sins of the world. Blessed are those who are called to the Supper of the Lamb.

COMMUNION OF THE SICK - SHORTER RITE

The People respond together with the Minister, once or three times:

Lord, I am not worthy that thou shouldest come under my roof, but speak the word only, and my soul shall be healed.

Then shall the Minister distribute Holy Communion to the sick person, and to any assembled who are properly disposed to receive, with these words:

The Body of our Lord Jesus Christ, which was given for thee, preserve thy body and soul unto everlasting life.

Or:

The Body of Christ.

When the distribution of Holy Communion is over, the Minister purifies the pyx, unless he is to go immediately to another sick person and the Blessed Sacrament remains in the vessel.

After Communion, silence may be kept.

Then the Minister says Let us pray *and the Postcommunion Prayer:*

O LORD, holy Father almighty, everlasting God, we faithfully beseech thee that the most sacred Body of our Lord Jesus Christ thy Son, which our brother (sister) hath received, may avail for the everlasting healing both of body and soul; through Jesus Christ our Lord.

The People respond: **Amen.**

Blessing

28. Then, if a Priest be the Minister, he may give the blessing by making, with the pyx, in silence, the Sign of the Cross. Otherwise the blessing is given verbally, as usual:

The Priest says:

> The Lord be with you.

People: **And with thy spirit.**

The peace of God, which passeth all understanding, keep your hearts and minds in the knowledge and love of God, and of his Son Jesus Christ our Lord; and the blessing of God Almighty, ✠ the Father, the Son, and the Holy Spirit, be amongst you, and remain with you always.

People: **Amen.**

In the absence of a Priest or Deacon, the Minister shall conclude as follows:

THE Almighty Lord, who is a most strong tower to all those who put their trust in him, to whom all things in heaven, in earth, and under the earth, do bow and obey; be now and evermore thy defence; and make thee know and feel, that there is none other Name under heaven given to man, in whom, and through whom, thou mayest receive health and salvation, but only the Name of our Lord Jesus Christ. **Amen.**

COMMUNION OF THE SICK - SHORTER RITE

A lay minister may say, while tracing the Sign of the Cross on the sick person's forehead:

UNTO God's gracious mercy and protection we commit thee. The Lord bless thee, and keep thee. The Lord make his face to shine upon thee, and be gracious unto thee. The Lord lift up his countenance upon thee, and give thee peace, both now and evermore. **Amen.**

CHAPTER FIVE:
ANOINTING OF THE SICK OUTSIDE OF MASS

Outline of the Rite

>Introductory Rites
>Penitential Rite
>Liturgy of the Word
>Rite of Anointing
>Blessing

29. The ordinary Minister of the Anointing the Sick is a Priest. Before anointing a sick person, the Priest should inquire about his (her) condition in order to plan the celebration properly and to choose the appropriate biblical readings and prayers. Whenever it is necessary, the Priest should first hear the sacramental confession of the sick person; otherwise the Penitential Rite is said.

The Anointing of the Sick should be administered to those who dangerously ill due to sickness or old age. A prudent or probable judgement about the seriousness of the sickness is sufficient.

A sick person should be anointed before surgery whenever a dangerous illness is the reason for the surgery. Old people may be anointed if they are in weak condition although no dangerous illness is present. Sick children may be anointed if they have sufficient use of reason to be comforted by this sacrament.

The sacrament may be repeated if the sick person recovers after anointing or if, during the same illness, the danger becomes more serious.

Introductory Rites

On entering the house or room, the Priest says:

        Peace be to this house, and to all that dwell in it.

People: **Amen.**

Or:

        The peace of the Lord be always with you.

People: **And with thy spirit.**

He then places the Oil Stock on the table prepared, and vests in a surplice and violet stole, or at least the stole.

30. Next the Priest may take the vessel of holy water and sprinkle the sick person and room, saying:

Thou shalt purge me with hyssop, O Lord, and I shall be clean; thou shalt wash me, and I shall be whiter than snow.

Priest: Our help is in the Name of the Lord.

People: **Who hath made heaven and earth.**

Priest: The Lord be with you.

People: **And with thy spirit.**

Priest: Let us pray.

O BLESSED Redeemer, relieve, we beseech thee, by thy indwelling power, the distress of this thy servant; release him (her) from sin, and drive away all pain of soul and body, that being restored to soundness of health, he (she) may offer thee praise and thanksgiving; who livest and reignest with the Father and the Holy Spirit, ever one God, world without end. **Amen.**

Penitential Rite

31. The Priest may then approach the sick person in order to ascertain if the person wishes to make his (her) confession. If so, wearing a violet stole, he shall hear his (her) confession and give absolution.

Unless the Sacrament of Penance has been celebrated, the Priest shall then proceed with the Penitential Rite.

Ye that do truly and earnestly repent you of your sins, and are in love and charity with your neighbours, and intend to lead a new life, following the commandments of God, and walking from henceforth in his holy ways: draw near with faith, and make your humble confession to almighty God, meekly kneeling upon your knees.

Or:

Let us humbly confess our sins unto Almighty God.

The People kneel, if they are able. Silence may be kept, and then the Priest begins as follows and the People join in saying:

**ALMIGHTY God,
Father of our Lord Jesus Christ,
maker of all things, judge of all men:**

We acknowledge and bewail our manifold sins
   and wickedness,
which we from time to time most grievously
   have committed,
by thought, word, and deed, against thy divine majesty,
provoking most justly thy wrath and indignation
   against us.

We do earnestly repent,
and are heartily sorry for these our misdoings;
the remembrance of them is grievous unto us,
the burden of them is intolerable.

Have mercy upon us,
have mercy upon us, most merciful Father;
for thy Son our Lord Jesus Christ's sake,
forgive us all that is past;
and grant that we may ever hereafter
serve and please thee in newness of life,
to the honour and glory of thy Name;
through Jesus Christ our Lord. Amen.

The Priest says:

May Almighty God, our heavenly Father, who of his great mercy hath promised forgiveness of sins to all those who with hearty repentance and true faith turn unto him, have mercy on us, pardon and deliver us from all our sins, confirm and strengthen us in all goodness, and bring us to everlasting life; through Jesus Christ our Lord. Amen.

ANOINTING OF THE SICK OUTSIDE OF MASS

Liturgy of the Word

32. Then, all standing who are able, the Priest may proclaim the Gospel, first saying with hands joined:

>The Lord be with you.

People: **And with thy spirit.**

A reading from the holy Gospel according to Matthew.   8:5-10,13

People: **Glory be to thee, O Lord.**

When Jesus entered Capernaum, a centurion came forward to him, beseeching him and saying, "Lord, my servant is lying paralyzed at home, in terrible distress." And he said to him, "I will come and heal him." But the centurion answered him, "Lord, I am not worthy to have you come under my roof; but only say the word, and my servant will be healed. For I am a man under authority, with soldiers under me; and I say to one, 'Go,' and he goes, and to another, 'Come,' and he comes, and to my slave, 'Do this,' and he does it." When Jesus heard him, he marvelled, and said to those who followed him, "Truly, I say to you, not even in Israel have I found such faith. And to the centurion Jesus said, "Go; be it done for you as you have believed." And the servant was healed at that very moment.

After the Gospel, Priest says:

>The Gospel of the Lord.

People: **Praise be to thee, O Christ.**

Rite of Anointing

33. The Priest begins the Rite of Anointing with the following invocations:

Priest: Lord have mercy upon us.
People: **Christ have mercy upon us.**
Priest: Lord have mercy upon us.

Priest: Lord, that thou wouldst visit and strengthen this sick man (woman).
People: **We beseech thee to hear us, good Lord.**

Priest: That thou wouldst grant him (her) life and health.
People: **We beseech thee to hear us, good Lord.**

Priest: That thou wouldst grant him (her) the grace of the Holy Spirit.
People: **We beseech thee to hear us, good Lord.**

Priest: O Lamb of God, that takest away the sins of the world.
People: **Spare us, O Lord.**

Priest: O Lamb of God, that takest away the sins of the world.
People: **Graciously hear us, O Lord.**

Priest: O Lamb of God, that takest away the sins of the world.
People: **Have mercy upon us.**

ANOINTING OF THE SICK OUTSIDE OF MASS

In silence, the Priest lays his hands on the head of the sick person. Before anointing the sick person, the Priest may say the following:

In the Name of the Father, ✠ and of the Son, ✠ and of the Holy ✠ Spirit, may there be extinguished in thee all power of the devil, through the imposition of our hands, and through the invocation of the glorious and holy Virgin Mary Mother of God, and of her illustrious Spouse Joseph, and of all holy Angels, Archangels, Patriarchs, Prophets, Apostles, Martyrs, Confessors and Virgins, and of all the Saints. Amen.

The Priest anoints the sick person with the Oil of the Sick. He anoints the forehead and hands, saying:

Through this holy anointing, may the Lord in his love and mercy help you with the grace of the Holy Spirit. **Amen.**

May the Lord who frees you from sin save you and raise you up. **Amen.**

The Priest may also anoint additional parts of the body. He does not repeat the sacramental formula.

He then says the following:

Priest: Lord, have mercy upon us.
People: **Christ, have mercy upon us.**
Priest: Lord, have mercy upon us.

Priest and People together:

OUR Father, who art in heaven, hallowed be thy Name, thy kingdom come, thy will be done, on earth as it is in heaven. Give us this day our daily bread. And forgive us our trespasses, as we forgive those who trespass against us. And lead us not into temptation, but deliver us from evil. Amen.

Priest: O Lord, save thy servant.
People: **Who putteth his (her) trust in thee.**

Priest: Send him (her) help from thy holy place;.
People: **And evermore mightily defend him (her).**

Priest: Let the enemy have no advantage of him (her);
People: **Nor the wicked approach to hurt him (her).**

Priest: Be unto him (her), O Lord, a strong tower;
People: **From the face of his (her) enemy.**

Priest: O Lord, hear our prayer.
People: **And let our cry come unto thee.**

Priest: The Lord be with you.
People: **And with thy spirit.**

Let us pray.

O LORD God, who by thy holy Apostle James hast said: Is any sick among you? Let him call for the priests of the Church; and let them pray over him, anointing him with oil in the Name of the Lord: and

ANOINTING OF THE SICK OUTSIDE OF MASS

the prayer of faith shall save the sick, and the Lord shall raise him up: and if he have committed sins they shall be forgiven him; heal, we beseech thee, O our Redeemer, by the grace of the Holy Spirit the weakness of this sick person, cure his (her) wounds, forgive his (her) sins, and cast out from him (her) of all pain of mind and body, mercifully restore unto him (her) soundness both within and without, that made whole by thy gracious aid, he (she) may return again to his (her) former course of life; who with the Father and the same Holy Spirit, livest and reignest ever one God, world without end. **Amen.**

34. If the sick person is to receive Communion, the Priest proceeds using the Rite of Holy Communion from the Communion of the Sick (Pg. 37).

35. The Priest concludes with a blessing as follows:

> The Lord be with you.

People: **And with thy spirit.**

The peace of God, which passeth all understanding, keep your hearts and minds in the knowledge and love of God, and of his Son Jesus Christ our Lord; and the blessing of God Almighty, ✠ the Father, the Son, and the Holy Spirit, be amongst you, and remain with you always.

People: **Amen.**

CHAPTER SIX:
PENANCE, ANOINTING, AND VIATICUM

(CONTINUOUS RITE FOR EXCEPTIONAL CIRCUMSTANCES AND FOR THOSE NEAR DEATH)

Outline of the Rite

Introductory Rites
Penitential Rite
Profession of Faith
Rite of Anointing
Communion as Viaticum
Blessing

36. For special cases, when sudden illness or some other cause has placed one of the faithful in danger of death, this continuous rite is provided by which the sick person may be given the sacraments of Penance, Anointing, and the Holy Eucharist as Viaticum in one service.

If death is near and there is not enough time to administer the three sacraments together, the sick person should be given an opportunity to make a sacramental confession. Then he (she) should be given Viaticum immediately. Afterwards, if there is sufficient time, the sick person is to be anointed. If because of his (her) illness, the sick person cannot receive Holy Communion, he (she) should be anointed.

Introductory Rites

On entering the house or room, the Priest says:

>Peace be to this house, and to all that dwell in it.

People: **Amen.**

Or:

>The peace of the Lord be always with you.

People: **And with thy spirit.**

Next the Priest may take the vessel of holy water and sprinkle the sick person and room, saying:

Thou shalt purge me with hyssop, O Lord, and I shall be clean; thou shalt wash me, and I shall be whiter than snow.

Priest: Our help is in the Name of the Lord.
People: **Who hath made heaven and earth.**

Priest: O Lord, hear my prayer.
People: **And let me cry come unto thee.**

Priest: The Lord be with you.
People: **And with thy spirit.**

Priest: Let us pray.

O LORD, holy Father, Almighty, everlasting God, we beseech thee to hear us; and vouchsafe to send thy holy Angel from heaven, to guard and cherish, protect and visit, and evermore defend all who are assembled in this place; through Christ our Lord. **Amen.**

Penitential Rite

37. The Priest may then approach the sick person in order to ascertain if the person wishes to make his (her) confession. If so, wearing a violet stole, he shall hear his (her) confession and absolve him (her).

Unless the Sacrament of Penance has been celebrated, the Priest shall then proceed with the Penitential Rite:

Ye that do truly and earnestly repent you of your sins, and are in love and charity with your neighbours, and intend to lead a new life, following the commandments of God, and walking from henceforth in his holy ways: draw near with faith, and make your humble confession to almighty God, meekly kneeling upon your knees.

The People kneel, if they are able. Silence may be kept, and then the Priest begins as follows and the People join in saying:

ALMIGHTY God,
Father of our Lord Jesus Christ,
  maker of all things, judge of all men:

We acknowledge and bewail our manifold sins
  and wickedness,
which we from time to time most grievously
  have committed,
by thought, word, and deed, against thy divine majesty,
provoking most justly thy wrath and indignation
  against us.

We do earnestly repent,
and are heartily sorry for these our misdoings;
the remembrance of them is grievous unto us,
the burden of them is intolerable.

Have mercy upon us,
have mercy upon us, most merciful Father;
for thy Son our Lord Jesus Christ's sake,
forgive us all that is past;
and grant that we may ever hereafter
serve and please thee in newness of life,
to the honour and glory of thy Name;
through Jesus Christ our Lord. Amen.

The Priest says:

May Almighty God, our heavenly Father, who of his great mercy hath promised forgiveness of sins to all those who with hearty repentance and true faith turn unto him, have mercy on us, pardon and deliver us from all our sins, confirm and strengthen us in all goodness, and bring us to everlasting life; through Jesus Christ our Lord. Amen.

At the conclusion of the Sacrament of Penance or the Penitential Rite, the Priest may give the Apostolic Pardon for the dying:

By the authority which the Apostolic See has given me, I grant you a full pardon and the remission of all your sins in the Name of the Father, and of the Son, ✠ and of the Holy Spirit. Amen.

Profession of Faith

38. If time allows and if the condition of the sick person permits, the baptismal profession of faith follows. The Minister first says and then asks the following questions:

Let us profess our faith in the redeeming love of God.

N., do you believe in God the Father Almighty, Maker of heaven and earth?

Sick person: **I do.**

Minister: Do you believe in Jesus Christ, his only Son our Lord, who was conceived by the Holy Ghost, born of the Virgin Mary, suffered under Pontius Pilate, was crucified, dead, and buried; he descended into hell; the third day he rose again from the dead; he ascended into heaven, and sitteth on the right hand of God the Father Almighty; from thence he shall come to judge the quick and the dead?

Sick person: **I do.**

Minister: Do you believe in the Holy Ghost; the holy Catholic Church; the Communion of Saints; the forgiveness of sins, the resurrection of the body, and the life everlasting?

Sick person: **All this I steadfastly believe.**

Rite of Anointing

39. The Priest begins the Rite of Anointing with the following invocations:

Priest: Lord have mercy upon us.
People: **Christ have mercy upon us.**
Priest: Lord have mercy upon us.

Priest: Lord, that thou wouldst visit and strengthen this sick man (woman).
People: **We beseech thee to hear us, good Lord.**

Priest: That thou wouldst grant him (her) life and health.
People: **We beseech thee to hear us, good Lord.**

Priest: That thou wouldst grant him (her) the grace of the Holy Spirit.
People: **We beseech thee to hear us, good Lord.**

Priest: O Lamb of God, that takest away the sins of the world.
People: **Spare us, O Lord.**

Priest: O Lamb of God, that takest away the sins of the world.
People: **Graciously hear us, O Lord.**

Priest: O Lamb of God, that takest away the sins of the world.
People: **Have mercy upon us.**

PENANCE, ANOINTING, AND VIATICUM

In silence, the Priest lays his hands on the head of the sick person. Before anointing the sick person, the Priest may say the following:

In the Name of the Father, ✠ and of the ✠ Son, and of the Holy ✠ Spirit, may there be extinguished in thee all power of the devil, through the imposition of our hands, and through the invocation of the glorious and holy Virgin Mary Mother of God, and of her illustrious Spouse Joseph, and of all holy Angels, Archangels, Patriarchs, Prophets, Apostles, Martyrs, Confessors and Virgins, and of all the Saints. Amen.

The Priest anoints the sick person with the Oil of the Sick. He anoints the forehead and hands, saying:

Through this holy anointing, may the Lord in his love and mercy help you with the grace of the Holy Spirit. Amen.

May the Lord who frees you from sin save you and raise you up. Amen.

The Priest may also anoint additional parts of the body. He does not repeat the sacramental formula.

Communion as Viaticum

40. *The Priest joins his hands to say:*

As our Saviour Christ hath commanded and taught us, we are bold to say,

And here he extends his hands and begins the Lord's Prayer, as the People continue with him:

And here he extends his hands and begins the Lord's Prayer, as the People continue with him:

OUR Father, who art in heaven, hallowed be thy Name, thy kingdom come, thy will be done, on earth as it is in heaven. Give us this day our daily bread. And forgive us our trespasses, as we forgive those who trespass against us. And lead us not into temptation, but deliver us from evil. Amen.

Then the Priest, bowing profoundly, may say with all who shall receive Communion:

WE do not presume to come to this thy Table, O merciful Lord, trusting in our own righteousness, but in thy manifold and great mercies.

We are not worthy so much as to gather up the crumbs under thy Table.

But thou art the same Lord whose property is always to have mercy.

Grant us therefore, gracious Lord,
so to eat the flesh of thy dear Son Jesus Christ,
and to drink his Blood,
that our sinful bodies may be made clean by his Body,
and our souls washed through his most precious Blood,
and that we may evermore dwell in him, and he in us.
Amen.

PENANCE, ANOINTING, AND VIATICUM

The Priest genuflects, takes the Host and, turning to the People, holding it slightly raised above the pyx, says aloud:

Behold the Lamb of God, behold him that taketh away the sins of the world. Blessed are those who are called to the Supper of the Lamb.

The People respond together with the Priest, once or three times:

Lord, I am not worthy that thou shouldest come under my roof, but speak the word only, and my soul shall be healed.

Then the Priest gives Holy Communion to the sick person, if by way of Viaticum with these words:

Receive, brother (sister), this food for thy journey, the Body of our Lord Jesus Christ, and may he preserve thee from the malicious enemy and bring thee to everlasting life. Amen.

If not by way of Viaticum then with these words:

The Body of our Lord Jesus Christ, which was given for thee, preserve thy body and soul unto everlasting life.

Or:

The Body of Christ.

When the distribution of Holy Communion is over, the Priest purifies the pyx, unless he is to go immediately to another sick person and the Blessed Sacrament remains in the vessel.

After Communion, silence may be kept.

Then the Priest standing and the People kneeling, if they are able, the Priest alone, or the Priest and the People together, may say the following:

ALMIGHTY and everliving God,
   we most heartily thank thee for that thou dost feed us,
in these holy mysteries,
with the spiritual food of the most precious Body and Blood
of thy Son our Saviour Jesus Christ;
and dost assure us thereby
of thy favour and goodness towards us;

and that we are very members incorporate
in the mystical body of thy Son,
the blessed company of all faithful people;

and are also heirs, through hope,
of thy everlasting kingdom,
by the merits of the most precious death and Passion
of thy dear Son.

And we humbly beseech thee, O heavenly Father,
so to assist us with thy grace,
that we may continue in that holy fellowship,
and do all such good works
as thou hast prepared for us to walk in;

through Jesus Christ our Lord,
to whom, with thee and the Holy Spirit,
be all honour and glory, world without end. Amen.

Then the Priest says Let us pray and the Postcommunion Prayer:

GOD of all grace and power: behold, visit, and relieve thy servant N.; look upon him (her) with the eyes of thy mercy; give him (her) comfort and sure confidence in thee, defend him (her) in all danger, and keep him (her) in perpetual peace and safety; through Jesus Christ thy Son our Lord, who liveth and reigneth with thee, in the unity of the Holy Spirit, ever one God, world without end.

The People respond: **Amen.**

Blessing

40. Then, in silence, the blessing is given by making, with the pyx, the Sign of the Cross. Otherwise the blessing is given verbally, as usual:

The Priest says:

> The Lord be with you.

People: **And with thy spirit.**

The peace of God, which passeth all understanding, keep your hearts and minds in the knowledge and love of God, and of his Son Jesus Christ our Lord; and the blessing of God Almighty, ✠ the Father, the Son, and the Holy Spirit, be amongst you, and remain with you always.

People: **Amen.**

CHAPTER SEVEN:
SUPPLICATION FOR THE DYING AND COMMENDATION OF A SOUL

41. It is the responsibility of Priests and Deacons, whenever possible, to assist the dying person and those who are with him and to recite the prayers of commendation and the prayer after death. When a Priest or Deacon is unable to be present because of other serious pastoral obligations, he should instruct the laity to assist the dying by reciting all such prayers as contained in this section that are expedient.

It is a devout custom that a lighted candle burn during the prayers for the dying, if at all possible.

On entering the house or room, the Minister may say these or other words of holy Scripture:

Thou wilt keep him in perfect peace whose mind is stayed on thee. *(Isaiah 26:3)*

Comfort the soul of thy servant; for unto thee, O Lord, do I lift up my soul. *(Psalm 86:4)*

The Lord is my light and my salvation; whom then shall I fear? The Lord is the strength of my life; of whom then shall I be afraid? *(Psalm 27:1)*

Yea, though I walk through the valley of the shadow of death, I will fear no evil; for thou art with me; thy rod and thy staff comfort me. *(Psalm 23:4)*

Let not your heart be troubled: ye believe in God, believe also in me. In my Father's house are many mansions. I go to prepare a place for you. And if I go and prepare a place for you, I will come again, and receive you unto myself; that where I am, there ye may be also. *(John 14:1-3)*

Into thy hands I commend my spirit; for thou hast redeemed me, O LORD, thou God of truth. *(Psalm 31:6)*

If a Priest or Deacon is present, he may take the vessel of holy water and sprinkle the sick person and the room, saying:

Thou shalt purge me with hyssop, O Lord, and I shall be clean; thou shalt wash me, and I shall be whiter than snow.

Litany for the Dying

O GOD the Father;	**Graciously hear us.**
O God the Son;	**Graciously hear us.**
O God the Holy Spirit;	**Graciously hear us.**
O Holy Trinity, one God;	**Graciously hear us.**
Holy Mary,	**pray for him (her).**
Saint Joseph,	**pray for him (her).**
All ye Angels and Saints,	**pray for him (her).**

Behold, O Lord, this thy servant, and in thy loving mercy,
Good Lord, deliver him (her).

SUPPLICATION FOR THE DYING

From darkness and doubt, **Good Lord, deliver him (her)**.
By thy holy Incarnation, **Good Lord, deliver him (her)**.
By thy Cross and Passion,**Good Lord, deliver him (her)**.
By thy Death and glorious Resurrection,
Good Lord, deliver him (her).

We sinners do beseech thee to hear us, O Lord God:
and that it may please thee to pardon all his (her) sins,
We beseech thee, good Lord.
To receive him (her) to thyself,
We beseech thee, good Lord.
To grant him (her) a place of refreshment, light, and peace
We beseech thee, good Lord.
To give him (her) joy and gladness in thy kingdom with thy Saints in light, **We beseech thee, good Lord.**
To bring him (her) into thine eternal glory,
We beseech thee, good Lord.
Assist him (her) in his (her) last agony.
We beseech thee, good Lord.

O Lamb of God, that takest away the sins of the world;
Have mercy upon him (her).
O Lamb of God, that takest away the sins of the world;
Have mercy upon him (her).
O Lamb of God, that takest away the sins of the world;
Grant him (her) thy peace.

Minister and People together:

OUR Father, who art in heaven, hallowed be thy Name, thy kingdom come, thy will be done, on earth as it is in heaven. Give us this day our daily bread. And forgive us our trespasses, as we forgive those who trespass against us. And lead us not into temptation, but deliver us from evil. Amen.

HAIL Mary, full of grace, the Lord is with thee; blessed art thou among women, and blessed is the fruit of thy womb Jesus. Holy Mary, Mother of God, pray for us sinners, now and at the hour of our death. Amen.

The Minister may continue:

Let us pray.

O SOVEREIGN Lord, who desirest not the death of a sinner: we beseech thee to loose the spirit of this thy servant from every bond, and set him (her) free all evil; that he (she) may rest with all thy Saints in the eternal habitations; through Jesus Christ our Lord, who liveth and reigneth with thee and the Holy Spirit, ever one God, world without end. **Amen.**

Salve Regina

HAIL, holy Queen, Mother of mercy; Hail, our life, our sweetness, and our hope. To thee do we cry, poor banished children of Eve; to thee do we send up our sighs, mourning and weeping in this vale of tears.

SUPPLICATION FOR THE DYING

Turn then, most gracious advocate, thine eyes of mercy towards us; and after this our exile, show unto us the blessed fruit of thy womb, Jesus. O clement, O loving, O sweet Virgin Mary.

V. Pray for us, O holy Mother of God.

R. **That we may be made worthy of the promises of Christ.**

Let us pray:

ALMIGHTY and everlasting God, who by the cooperation of the Holy Ghost, didst prepare the body and soul of the glorious Virgin Mother Mary to become a habitation meet for thy Son: Grant that as we rejoice in her commemoration, we may be delivered by her loving intercession from our present evils and from eternal death; through the same Christ our Lord. **Amen.**

42. When the moment of death seems to be at hand, the Minister or another should say the following:

Commendatory Prayers at Death

Proficiscere

GO forth, O Christian soul, from this world, in the Name of God the omnipotent Father who created thee; in the Name of Jesus Christ, the Son of the living God, who suffered for thee; in the Name of the Holy Ghost, who hath been poured out on thee; in the name of the glorious and holy Virgin Mary, Mother of God; in the name of Blessed Joseph, her Spouse most chaste; in the name of Angels, and Archangels; in the name of Thrones and Dominations; in the name of Princedoms and of Powers; in the name of Virtues, Cherubim and Seraphim; in the name of Patriarchs and Prophets, in the name of holy Apostles and Evangelists; in the name of holy Martyrs and Confessors; in the name of holy Monks and Hermits; in the name of holy Virgins and of all the Saints of God, both men and women. May thy rest be this day in peace, and thy dwelling-place in holy Sion: through the same Christ our Lord. **Amen.**

Or:

DEPART, O Christian soul, out of this world, in the Name of God the Father Almighty who created thee. In the Name of Jesus Christ who redeemed thee. In the Name of the Holy Ghost who sanctifieth thee. May thy rest be this day in peace, and thy dwelling place in the Paradise of God. **Amen.**

When the soul has departed, the following shall be prayed:

O ALMIGHTY God, with whom do live the spirits of just men made perfect: We humbly commend this thy servant, our dear brother (sister), into thy hands, as into the hands of a faithful Creator, and most merciful Saviour. Wash him (her), we pray thee, in the blood of the immaculate Lamb, that was slain to take away the

SUPPLICATION FOR THE DYING

sin of the world; that whatsoever defilements he (she) may have contracted in the midst of this wicked world, through the lusts of the flesh or the wiles of Satan, being purged and done away, he (she) may be presented pure and without spot before thee; through the merits of Jesus Christ thine only Son our Lord. **Amen.**

NOW unto him that is able to keep us from falling and to present us faultless before the presence of his glory with exceeding joy; to the only wise God our Saviour be glory and majesty, dominion and power, both now and ever. **Amen.**

Or:

INTO thy hands, O merciful Saviour, we commend the soul of thy servant, now departed from the body. Acknowledge, we humbly beseech thee, a sheep of thine own fold, a lamb of thine own flock, a sinner of thine own redeeming. Receive him (her) into the arms of thy mercy, into the blessed rest of everlasting peace, and into the glorious company of the Saints in light. **Amen.**

CHAPTER EIGHT:
ADDITIONAL PRAYERS

FOR THE SICK

For patience in affliction

ALMIGHTY and everlasting God, who, of thy tender love towards mankind, hast sent thy Son our Saviour Jesus Christ, to take upon him our flesh, and to suffer death upon the cross, that all mankind should follow the example of his great humility: Mercifully grant, that we may both follow the example of his patience, and also be made partakers of his Resurrection; through the same Jesus Christ our Lord. **Amen.**

For strength in the Holy Spirit

O GOD, the protector of all that trust in thee: Grant, we beseech thee, to this thy servant, that he (she) may be sustained and sanctified by thy Holy Spirit, and strengthened in soul and body; through Jesus Christ our Lord. **Amen.**

For trust in the presence of God

ALMIGHTY God, giver of health and healing: Grant to this thy servant such a sense of thy presence that he (she) may have perfect trust in thee. In all his (her) suffering may he (she) cast his (her) care upon thee, so that, enfolded in thy love and power, he (she) may receive from thee health and salvation according to thy gracious will; through Jesus Christ our Lord. **Amen.**

For healing gifts

ALMIGHTY and immortal God, the giver of life and health: We beseech thee to hear our prayers for thy servant N., for whom we implore thy mercy, that by thy blessing upon him (her) and upon those who minister to him (her) of thy healing gifts, he (she) may be restored, according to thy gracious will, to health of body and mind, and give thanks to thee in thy holy Church; through Jesus Christ our Lord. **Amen.**

Before an operation

ALMIGHTY Father, giver of life and health: Look mercifully, we beseech thee, on the sick and suffering, especially this thy servant for whom our prayers are desired, that by thy blessing upon him (her) and upon those who minister to him (her), he (she) may be restored, if it be thy gracious will, to health of body and mind, and give thanks to thee in thy Holy Church; through Jesus Christ our Lord. **Amen.**

ADDITIONAL PRAYERS

For recovery of health

O FATHER of mercies and God of all comfort, our only help in time of need: We humbly beseech thee to behold, visit, and relieve thy sick servant (N.) for whom our prayers are desired. Look upon him (her) with the eyes of thy mercy; comfort him (her) with a sense of thy goodness; preserve him (her) from the temptations of the enemy; and give him (her) patience under his (her) affliction. In thy good time, restore him (her) to health, and enable him (her) to lead the remainder of his (her) life in thy fear, and to thy glory; and grant that finally he (she) may dwell with thee in life everlasting; through Jesus Christ our Lord. **Amen.**

For strength and comfort

O MERCIFUL God, and heavenly Father, who hast taught us in thy holy word that thou dost not willingly afflict or grieve the children of men: Look with pity, we beseech thee, upon the sorrows of thy servant for whom our prayers are offered. Remember him (her), O Lord, in mercy; endue his (her) soul with patience; comfort him (her) with a sense of thy goodness; lift up thy countenance upon him (her), and give him (her) peace; through Jesus Christ our Lord. **Amen.**

For comfort in suffering

ALMIGHTY God our heavenly Father: We beseech thee graciously to comfort thy servant in his (her) suffering, and to bless the means made use of for his (her) cure. Fill his (her) heart with confidence, that though he (she) be sometime afraid, he (she) yet may put his (her) trust in thee; through Jesus Christ our Lord. **Amen.**

For those in anxiety and distress

ALMIGHTY God, who art afflicted in the afflictions of thy people: Regard with thy tender compassion those in anxiety and distress; bear their sorrows and their cares; supply all their manifold needs; and help both them and us to put our whole trust and confidence in thee; through Jesus Christ our Lord. **Amen.**

For loving mercy and restoration of health

HEAR us, Almighty and most merciful God and Saviour: Extend thy accustomed goodness to this thy servant who is grieved with sickness. Visit him (her), O Lord, with thy loving mercy, and so restore him (her) to his (her) former health, that he (she) may give thanks unto thee in thy holy Church; through Jesus Christ our Lord. **Amen.**

For sanctification in sickness and strength in faith

SANCTIFY, we beseech thee, O Lord, the sickness of this thy servant: that the sense of his (her) weakness may add strength to his (her) faith, and seriousness to his (her) repentance; and grant that he (she) may dwell with thee in life everlasting; through Jesus Christ our Lord. **Amen.**

For merciful consolation

HEAR, O Lord, we beseech thee, these our prayers, as we call upon thee on behalf of this thy servant; and bestow upon him (her) the help of thy merciful consolation; through Jesus Christ our Lord. **Amen.**

For recovery from sickness

O GOD, the strength of the weak and the comfort of sufferers: Mercifully accept our prayers, and grant to thy servant the help of thy power, that his (her) sickness may be turned into health, and our sorrow into joy; through Jesus Christ our Lord. **Amen.**

For recovery from sickness

O GOD of heavenly powers, who, by the might of thy command, canst drive away from men's bodies all sickness and all infirmity: Be present in thy goodness with this thy servant, that his (her) weakness may be banished and his (her) strength recalled; that his (her) health being thereupon restored, he (she) may bless thy holy Name; through Jesus Christ our Lord. **Amen.**

For the despondent and sorrowful

COMFORT, we beseech thee, most gracious God, this thy servant, cast down and faint of heart amidst the sorrows and difficulties of the world; and grant that, by the power of thy Holy Spirit, he (she) may be enabled to go upon his (her) way rejoicing, and give thee continual thanks for thy sustaining providence; through Jesus Christ our Lord. **Amen.**

For those in mental darkness

O HEAVENLY Father, we beseech thee to have mercy upon all thy children who are living in mental darkness. Restore them to strength of mind and cheerfulness of spirit, and give them health and peace; through Jesus Christ our Lord. **Amen.**

For a sick child

HEAVENLY Father, watch with us, we pray thee, over the sick child for whom our prayers are offered, and grant that he (she) may be restored to that perfect health which it is thine alone to give; through Jesus Christ our Lord. **Amen.**

For the convalescent

LORD, whose compassions fail not, and whose mercies are new every morning; we give thee hearty thanks that it hath pleased thee to give this our brother (sister) both relief from pain and hope of renewed health.

Continue, we beseech thee, in him (her) the good work that thou hast begun; that, daily increasing in bodily strength, and humbly rejoicing in thy goodness, he (she) may so order his (her) life as always to think and do such things as shall please thee; through Jesus Christ our Lord. **Amen**.

For those approaching death

O FATHER of mercies, and God of all comfort, our only help in time of need: We fly unto thee for succour on behalf of this thy servant, here lying in great weakness of body. Look graciously upon him (her), O Lord; and the more the outward man decayeth, strengthen him (her), we beseech thee, so much the more continually with thy grace and Holy Spirit in the inner man. Give him (her) unfeigned repentance for all the errors of his (her) life past, and steadfast faith in thy Son Jesus; that his (her) sins may be done away by thy mercy, and his (her) pardon sealed in heaven; through the same thy Son, our Lord and Saviour. **Amen**.

UNTO thee, O Lord, we commend the soul of thy servant N., that dying to the world, he (she) may live to thee; and whatsoever sins he (she) has committed through the frailty of earthly life, we beseech thee to do away by thy most loving and merciful forgiveness; through Jesus Christ our Lord. **Amen**.

O GOD, our heavenly Father, in whom we live and move and have our being: Grant to thy servant grace to desire only thy most holy will; that whether living or dying, he (she) may be thine; for his sake who loved us and gave himself for us, Jesus Christ our Lord. **Amen.**

For a holy death

O GOD, whose days are without end, and whose mercies cannot be numbered: Make us, we beseech thee, deeply sensible of the shortness and uncertainty of human life; and let thy Holy Spirit lead us in holiness and righteousness, all our days: that, when we shall have served thee in our generation, we may be gathered unto our fathers, having the testimony of a good conscience; in the communion of the Catholic Church; in the confidence of a certain faith; in the comfort of a reasonable, religious, and holy hope; in favour with thee our God, and in perfect charity with the world. All which we ask through Jesus Christ our Lord. **Amen.**

Additional prayers for the dying

THOU knowest, Lord, the secrets of our hearts; shut not thy merciful ears to our prayer; but spare us, Lord most holy, O God most mighty, O holy and merciful Saviour, thou most worthy Judge eternal, suffer us not, at our last hour, for any pains of death, to fall from thee. **Amen.**

ADDITIONAL PRAYERS

UNTO thee, O Lord, we commend the soul of thy servant N., that dying to the world he (she) may live unto thee; and whatsoever sins he (she) hath committed through the frailty of earthly life, we beseech thee to do away by thy most loving and merciful forgiveness; through Jesus Christ our Lord. **Amen.**

O GOD our heavenly Father, in whom we live and move and have our being: Grant to this thy servant grace to desire only thy most holy will; that whether living or dying he (she) may be thine; for his sake who loved us and gave himself for us, Jesus Christ our Lord. **Amen.**

O ALMIGHTY God, with whom do live the spirits of just men made perfect after they are delivered from their earthly prisons: We humbly commend the soul of this thy servant, our dear brother (sister), into thy hands, as into the hands of a faithful Creator, and most merciful Saviour; beseeching thee, that he (she) may be precious in thy sight. Wash him (her), we pray thee, in the blood of that immaculate Lamb, that was slain to take away the sins of the world; that whatsoever defilements he (she) may have contracted, through the lusts of the flesh or the wiles of Satan, being purged and done away, he (she) may be presented pure and without spot before thee; through the merits of Jesus Christ thine only Son our Lord. **Amen.**

ALMIGHTY and merciful God, who bestowest upon mankind both the remedies of health and the gifts of life everlasting: look mercifully upon thy servant N., now labouring under great weakness of body, and comfort the soul which thou hast created; so that at the hour of his (her) departure, he (she) may be presented without spot by the hands of thy holy Angels unto thee, his (her) Creator; through thy Son, Jesus Christ our Lord, who with thee, in the unity of the Holy Spirit, liveth and reigneth God, world without end. **Amen.**

WE beseech thee, Almighty God, mercifully to strengthen this thy servant N. by thy grace: that in the hour of death the adversary may not prevail against him (her), but that with thine Angels he (she) may enter into life eternal; through Jesus Christ our Lord. **Amen.**

For a dying child

O LORD Jesus Christ, the Only Begotten Son of God, who for our sakes didst become a babe in Bethlehem: We commit unto thy loving care this child whom thou art calling to thyself. Send thy holy Angel to lead him (her) gently to those heavenly habitations where the souls of those who sleep in thee have perpetual peace and joy, and fold him (her) in the everlasting arms of thine unfailing love; who livest and reignest with the Father and the Holy Ghost, one God world without end. **Amen.**

APPENDIX:
SACRAMENTAL AND OTHER FORMULAS

SACRAMENT OF PENANCE

The penitent makes the Sign of the Cross, saying:

In the Name of the Father, ✠ and of the Son, and of the Holy Spirit. Amen.

The Priest may say:

The Lord be in thy heart and on thy lips, that thou mayest truly confess thy sins to Almighty God.

The Penitent says:

Bless me, Father, for I have sinned. It has been … since my last confession. These are my sins: …

After the penitent confesses his (her) sins, the Priest gives counsel and appoints the penance. Then the penitent makes his (her) act of contrition with these or similar words:

O my God, I am heartily sorry for having offended thee, and I detest all my sins, because I dread the loss of heaven, and the pains of hell; but most of all because they offend thee, my God, who are all good and deserving of all my love. I firmly resolve, with the help of thy grace, to amend my life, to sin no more, and to avoid the near occasions of sin. Amen.

Or:

Lord Jesus, Son of God, have mercy on me, a sinner.

The Priest says the words of absolution:

God, the Father of mercies, through the Death and Resurrection of his Son, has reconciled the world to himself and sent the Holy Spirit among us for the forgiveness of sins; through the ministry of the Church may God give you pardon and peace, and I absolve you from your sins in the Name of the Father, ✠ and of the Son, and of the Holy Spirit.

The penitent answers: **Amen.**

The Priest may say these or similar words:

Blessed are those whose sins have been forgiven, whose evil deeds have been forgotten. Rejoice in the Lord, and go in peace.

Or:

May the Passion of Lord Jesus Christ, the intercession of the Blessed Virgin Mary and of all the Saints, whatever good thou shalt do and whatever suffering thou shalt endure, heal thy sins, help thee to grow in holiness, and bring thee to eternal life. Go in peace.

ANOINTING OF THE SICK

The Priest anoints the sick person with the Oil of the Sick. He anoints the forehead and hands, saying:

Through this holy anointing, may the Lord in his love and mercy help you with the grace of the Holy Spirit. Amen.

May the Lord who frees you from sin save you and raise you up. Amen.

The Priest may also anoint additional parts of the body. He does not repeat the sacramental formula.

VIATICUM

The Priest gives Holy Communion to the sick person by way of Viaticum with these words:

Receive, brother (sister), this food for thy journey, the Body of our Lord Jesus Christ, and may he preserve thee from the malicious enemy and bring thee to everlasting life. Amen.

APOSTOLIC PARDON

The Priest gives the Apostolic Pardon for the dying with these words:

By the authority which the Apostolic See has given me, I grant thee a full pardon and the remission of all thy sins in the Name of the Father, ✠ and of the Son, and of the Holy Spirit. **Amen.**